Introduction

Why let youngsters have a

Our God is a God of community and creativity. We need to live and die well and to ... glory, but innovative ways of helping us do this can be very hard to find. The traumas of bereavement, debilitating illness, loneliness and boredom may mean the loss of the will to live, even for Christians.

The activities in this manual have been used to bring many people 'back to life' and have opened the door of faith, sometimes for the very first time.

Soon after being seconded to a Nursing Home as a pastoral worker, I had an encounter with an elderly couple that was to change the direction of my ministry. Christine* still had a brilliant mind, although a massive stroke had left her visually impaired, with a maddeningly unresponsive body. Her husband Tom* also had little sight and being lethargic and withdrawn, seemed deep in depression. He described being in the Home as his worst possible nightmare. Christine sounded very bitter as she exclaimed about Tom, "You'll never ever, ever get him involved in anything!"

Her statement and their tragic situation haunted me because, naturally speaking, there seemed nothing that I could do, and yet deep down inside I believed that, with God's help, the impossible was possible.

So began my search to find something worthwhile for Tom and Christine to do. As I prayed for them one day, my eyes rested on several cube-shaped boxes I was saving. "We could make a large-scale word game similar to Boggle," I thought. Back at the Home I shared my idea with Christine and asked her to think of the best letters to use on the faces of the cubes. I covered all the boxes and inscribed them with the giant letters of her choice and we played our very first word game together. Before long Tom joined in!

Over time we built up an increasingly good relationship and developed more games and activities which now appear, with others, in this manual. At first Tom and Christine had no time for any talk of God, but to my delight things gradually changed and one day, shortly before he died, Tom, formerly an adamant atheist, told me that he had come to believe. The games that I have shared in the manual have in many ways been the springboard of my ministry.

'Fun with a purpose' sums it all up very neatly. It's really thrilling to see people reconnecting with life and, in some cases, finding spiritual help through these very simple games and activities.

This manual has a range of games and activities for use in Residential or Nursing Homes, or in people's own homes. Many were designed so that Visually Impaired People (VIPs) were on the same footing as their contemporaries.

Some games have been hand-made, as often they can be very expensive to buy. Involving people in the planning and making of them can be of enormous value. Feel free to improvise and customise so that they are appropriate for your clientele and their circumstances!

So, if you want to try some easy-to-do games and activities, then you will appreciate this new resource.

Have fun!

Sylvena Farrant

'I have come that they may have life, and have it to the full.' (John 10:10b)

*Not their real names

Acknowledgements

There are a number of people and organisations, too many to mention by name, without whose help, encouragement and prayers this manual would never have come into being.

I am especially indebted to David Heydon, the Director of Outlook Trust and his wife Judy who launched in me the idea of producing this manual after I had shared some of my games at their annual conference. Then, over many months, Judy in particular provided many hours of practical assistance in bringing things together.

My pastors at Bromley Baptist Church, Simon Jones and Brian Reed, and many of the congregation have inspired and encouraged me in various ways and I am especially thankful to Sue Hendrick and Mollie Kent who have been outstanding in their support and with the practical help they have given to me. I have also benefited enormously from being part of the wonderful team of helpers at the 'Holidays at Home for over 55's' at the church.

Diana Knights and Bromley Torch Fellowship Group for the Blind have also been very supportive.

The staff and residents of Mission Care's Elmwood Nursing Home have helped in many ways as this is where many of these ideas were birthed and tested as God answered my prayers of desperation to find worthwhile, inexpensive, things to do for people with multiple disabilities.

Most of all I would like thank the family of the London City Mission who have supported and encouraged me during over 40 years of ministry with them and especially after the death of my husband in 1994. They have also brought together the final production of this manual.

Sylvena Farrant
April 2009

There is a support page at www.lcm.org.uk/funwithapurpose where you will find tips on using this manual, any updates and an online forum.

Key to symbols

 Suitable for Visually Impaired People

 Games

 Activities and projects

 Talks

 Spiritual applications – to be used as and when appropriate

Contents

These pages have been especially designed for photocopying, and you have permission to make photocopies for use in practice.

However, this book is copyright and permission should be obtained from the London City Mission before reprinting or publishing any of this material.

Introduction

Games

Activities

Thoughts for Talks

Details of suppliers are provided. Prices are from March 2009 and are approximate.

GIANT SNAKES AND LADDERS

This giant Snakes and Ladders board can easily be put up on the wall.

Cut out and laminate different coloured circles, making them a little smaller than the squares on the board. Assign each player a colour and use Blu-tack to advance the piece around the board.

Use a large dice on an edged tray and get each player to take turns to roll the dice. A mobile person can then move the counters the necessary number of squares.

There are also larger garden versions of this game which can be used inside or out and which are fun to play with children.

Thoughts for talks *You can devise labels for each of the snakes and ladders to illustrate thoughts to discuss – snakes being bad, negative things and ladders being positive thoughts.*

Sylvena's jottings

SNAKES (DOWNS) OF LIFE

UNBELIEF Psalm 14:1 'The fool says in his heart, "There is no God." 2 Timothy 3:5 – 'having a form of godliness but denying its power.'

DISOBEDIENCE Hebrews 4:6 – 'did not go in, because of their disobedience.' Hebrews 2:3 – 'how shall we escape if we ignore such a great salvation?'

UNRESOLVED CONFLICT Lamentations 5:21 – 'Restore us to yourself, O Lord.'

JEALOUSY/ENVY Galatians 5:16-26 – Life by the Spirit. 'Envy, jealousy, malice and pride, they should never in my heart abide' – old chorus!

FAMILY BREAK-UP Hebrews 12:2 – 'Let us fix our eyes on Jesus…'

DEPRESSION Psalm 42:5 – 'Why are you downcast, O my soul? Put your hope in God.'

BEREAVEMENT 2 Corinthians 1:3 – 'the Father of compassion and the God of all comfort.'

SEVERE PAIN/DISABILITY Isaiah 53:2-12 – 'familiar with suffering… carried our sorrows… by his wounds we are healed.'

FEAR/WORRY Philippians 4:6 – 'do not be anxious about anything, but…'

PRIDE Proverbs 16:18 – 'Pride goes before destruction, a haughty spirit before a fall.' Ephesians 2:9 – 'not by works, so that no one can boast.'

LADDERS (UPS) OF LIFE

PRAYER Focus on God first, not our troubles. "More wrought by prayer than this world dreams of." (Alfred, Lord Tennyson). James 5:13 – 'Is any one of you in trouble? He should pray." 1 Thessalonians 5:17 – 'Pray continually.' Acts 1:14 – 'all… in prayer.'

HELPING HAND 'Stretcher-bearer' (see Mark 2:1-12). Galatians 6:2 – 'Carry each other's burdens.'

FELLOWSHIP "No man is an island" (John Donne). Hebrews 10:25 – 'Let us not give up meeting together.' Jesus to synagogue regularly. Acts 2:42 – 'devoted themselves to… fellowship.' Coal fire – take a coal away and it dies – put back with others and…

NURTURE/ENCOURAGEMENT 1 Thessalonians 5:11 – 'Encourage… build each other up…' Galatians 4:19 – 'the pains of childbirth until Christ is formed in you…'

BIBLE READING Jesus, Bread of Life (see John 6:35). Psalm 119:105 – 'light for my path.' Psalm 119:11 – keeps us from sin. "The Bible will keep you from sin, or sin will keep you from the Bible" (Dwight L Moody).

COUNTING YOUR BLESSINGS/THANKSGIVING Philippians 4:6 – 'in everything… with thanksgiving…' Psalm 95:2 – 'Let us come before him with thanksgiving.'

FORGIVENESS Matthew 6:15 – 'if you do not forgive men their sins, your Father will not forgive your sins. Hebrews 12:15 – 'no bitter root grows up to cause trouble.'

OBEDIENCE 1 Samuel 15:22 – To obey is better than sacrifice.'

HOLY LIVING Hebrews 12:14 – 'without holiness no one will see the Lord.' Matthew 5:16 – 'see your good deeds and praise your Father in heaven.'

GIANT NOUGHTS AND CROSSES

A game for two players or two teams. One player has the noughts, the other the crosses and they take it in turns to place one of these onto a square on the board.

The first one to get a row of 3 noughts or 3 crosses horizontally, vertically or diagonally is the winner.

GIANT FLOOR VERSION

People are placed round the edges if in wheelchairs and given the noughts and crosses to play as above. However, they have to throw them to the desired square and they count only if they land within the boundaries of the squares.

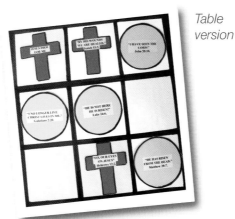

Table version

Large circles (representing the stone that was rolled away) and crosses with different Bible texts can be used to play the game instead of ordinary 'noughts' and 'crosses'. Yellow background for circles and red for crosses work well.

HOW TO MAKE

Snakes & Ladders
Best to buy this large format game, but you may also use a colour photocopier to enlarge a standard size board.

Noughts & Crosses
Make your own board by covering card with white sticky-back plastic (eg Contact). Use black PVC tape to mark out the board.

Make the noughts and crosses of a size that comfortably fits inside the squares. Use coloured card or paint them. When dry, laminate and cut out.

Bigger versions for the floor or outside can be made using two shades of carpet tiles, thick card, rope or garden canes for the lines. These can be coloured to make them stand out, and the original Os and Xs can be used.

COMMERCIAL SUPPLIERS

Big Game Hunters
Giant Snakes & Ladders (£35)
Tel: 08701 501 511
www.gardengames.co.uk

Marks and Spencer
Giant Noughts & Crosses Game (£15)
www.marksandspencer.com

Traditional Garden Games
Giant Snakes & Ladders (£40)

Giant Noughts & Crosses game (£15)

5-in-1 Game Set: includes Giant Snakes & Ladders, Giant Noughts & Crosses game, Giant Draughts board, Ring Quoits, and Giant Snakes & Ladders Puzzle (£30)

12 Racecourse Road
East Ayton
Scarborough
YO13 9HP

www.traditionalgardengames.co.uk

Thoughts for talks

Crosses...
- **at end of a letter to denote love** - *Love God, Love others, 'while we were still sinners Christ died for us' (Romans 5:8)*
- **denote that something is wrong** - *God forgives, yet – 'All have sinned and fall short of the glory of God' (Romans 3:23)*
- **are used when you vote for a person** - *Vote for Jesus – match up to Him*

3 in a row – **Jesus, with a criminal on either side of Him** - *yet one was saved, one was not – which side are we on?*

We are nothing (noughts) without Christ – *'I have been crucified with Christ and I no longer live but Christ lives in me.' (Galatians 2:20)*

*In noughts and crosses we are matching up, **trying to get a line of the same** – 'Do not conform any longer to the pattern of this world.' (Romans 12:2)*

How much do we stick to God's line in His Word? We mustn't change the rules or we will not know where we are! Plumb line in Amos 7:7-8, Isaiah 28:17 – Therefore 'Do not merely listen to the word... Do what it says.' (James 1:22)

Complete the game and win His approval to the end. 'Run with perseverance – fix our eyes on Jesus, the author and perfecter of our faith.' (Hebrews 12:1-2)

GIANT SOLITAIRE

A popular commercially produced game that is available in a larger size and is a good mind exercise for individuals.

HOW TO PLAY

Set up the board by placing all 32 balls in the holes, leaving the centre hole empty.

Remove the balls one by one by jumping over each other, to finish with one final ball in the centre hole.

Never jump diagonally, always horizontally or vertically. The jumped over ball is removed from the board.

Repeat until there are no more balls to jump over.

The game is over when the player cannot jump over any of the other balls and the game is won by landing on the centre hole with the final move.

GIANT 4-IN-A-ROW

A large and commercially produced game where the winner is the one who scores '4 in a row', either across, down or diagonally.

Thoughts for talks ✝

Life can seem full of obstacles to be jumped or leapt over and such a solitary game. Our God is able to help, if we let Him. He doesn't want us to go it alone.

Psalm 18:29 says '...by my God have I leaped over a wall.' (KJV)

Do we ask for God's help in getting over the obstacles we face?

✝ **Do our '4 in a row' as Christians – prayer, Bible reading, fellowship and telling others – match up to what they should be.**

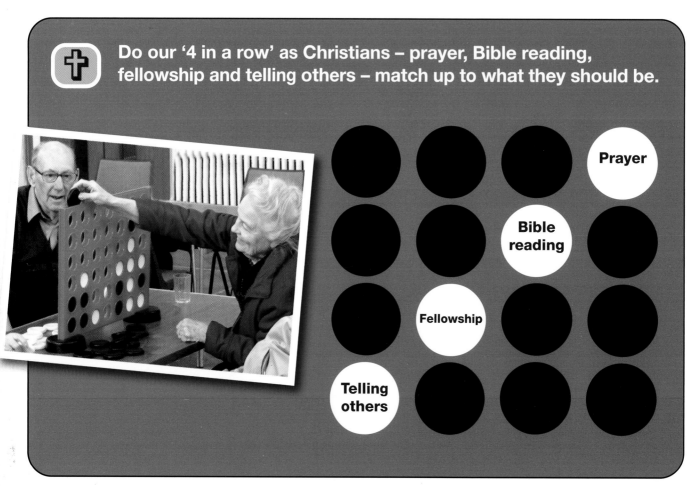

SHOVE HA'PENNY

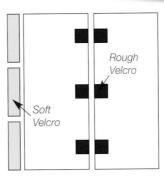

A fun giant game which is easy to make – and can be folded up for storage.

WHAT YOU NEED

1 large piece of thick white card
Black and red tape
Stick on Velcro
Different coloured card for circles
Self-adhesive clear covering film
Laminating sheets

HOW TO MAKE

Take a sheet of thick white card, cut in half lengthways to make it easy to store.

Stick red and black tape in lines as shown above. Ensure that all edges are well stuck down as any lips will interfere with the 'shove'. Cover each half of the card with the self-adhesive film, ensuring that you use one continuous piece – no joins!

Stick the rough velcro on the back of both sides of the white card to fix together, with the soft velcro over the top when playing (see diagram). Remove to store.

Make the coloured circles out of the different coloured cards, 3 for each player, and laminate so that they slide easily over the board. Ensure that these fit between the lines of the board.

Rough Velcro

Soft Velcro

*Rear view
(before velcro sealed)*

The game is now ready to play.

HOW TO PLAY

Each player takes it in turn to 'shove' their coloured circles up on the board by hitting, flipping or throwing the circles – whichever is best for the person concerned.

Each circle that rests within the black lines scores a point.

The first player to get 3 counters in any lined space is the winner.

COMMERCIAL SUPPLIERS

Big Game Hunters
Giant Connect 4 (£170)
Big 4 (£130)
Tel: 08701 501 511
www.gardengames.co.uk

The Garden Game Company
Floor Standing Connect 4 (£165)
Big 4 (£130)
www.thegardengame.co.uk

Time to Sow
Giant Four in a Row (£30)
Tel: 01462 639829
www.timetosow.com

Traditional Garden Games
Giant 4-in-a-Row (£30)
12 Racecourse Road
East Ayton
Scarborough
YO13 9HP
www.traditionalgardengames.co.uk

Garden Centre Online
Giant Four in a Row (£20)
Tel: 0845 094 3204
www.gardencentreonline.co.uk

Wooden Toys UK
Giant Wooden Solitaire Board (£50)
Tel: 0844 870 8697 or 0844 870 4263
www.woodentoys-uk.co.uk

Thoughts for talks ✝

Does anything 'shove us' along in life and if so, what?

What motivates us and gets us to 'have a go'; persist and persevere?

Does the love of Christ compel us?
(2 Corinthians 5:14)

What difference does the love of Christ in us make to our lives and that of others?

DOMINOES

DOMINOES CLASSIC

Game for 2–4 players, consisting of 28 giant dominoes.

Each player has 7 dominoes. A random domino is placed on the table and everyone takes it in turn to match the number dots – the winner is the first to use up all their dominoes.

There are variants on this classic game so follow the manufacturer's instructions.

> ## Thoughts for talks
> ***Do we follow our manufacturer's instructions?***
>
> *Exodus 20:1-17*
> *Matthew 22:37-39*

DOMINO ASCENT

Good option for visually impaired people!

Domino Ascent is played with the same rules as Dominoes Classic but instead of building outwards, players build up. By stacking the dominoes on top of each other they never go out of the field of vision of VIPs.

Keep the numbers to be matched pointing in the same direction as the tower gets higher – remove the lower dominoes if it begins to get too high.

Also great to play when there is not a large enough surface to play Dominoes Classic.

> ## Thoughts for talks
> ***Are we keen to get rid of all sin?***
> Jesus is the answer. *1 John 1:9*

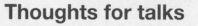

> ## Thoughts for talks
> ***On what or whom are we building our lives?***

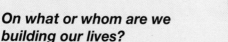

HOW TO MAKE

Make your own set of dominoes using rectangular pot scourers – these are cheap to make and thoroughly enjoyed by all who have played with them.

Simply apply white paint to hard surface of pot scourer (the darker green on the top the better). You will need 28, as in a normal set of dominoes.

Gentleman in Residential Home enjoying painting the dominoes

COMMERCIAL SUPPLIERS

Garden Selections
Giant Dominoes (£13)
28 lightweight foam dominoes
Boxed with carrying handle
www.selections.com

Traditional Garden Games
Jumbo Black & White Dominoes (£20)
12 Racecourse Road
East Ayton
Scarborough
YO13 9HP
www.traditionalgardengames.co.uk

Big Game Hunters
Giant Dominoes (£30)
Tel: 08701 501 511
www.gardengames.co.uk

TOPPLE DOMINOES

Stand the dominoes up on their edges, fairly close together – everyone can help.

Gently tip or blow the first domino over and watch them all fall down.

Experiment with different arrangements.

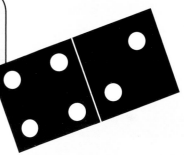

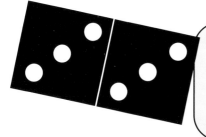

Thoughts for talks

Do we follow the crowd and then get lost?

Matthew 7:13-14

TOWER DOMINOES

Take it in turns to add a domino. See how tall a tower you can build before it all falls down.

Sing the song 'Build on the Rock' or 'The name of the Lord is a strong tower' as you build!

Ensure you use foam dominoes so that no-one is injured when they topple!

Thoughts for talks

How like the builders of the Tower of Babel are we? Genesis 11:1-9

There is a good range of popular games available to buy at a reasonable cost.

HOOPLA

Also known as 'Quoits'.

Lay the Hoopla base a suitable distance away, bearing in mind the abilities of the individual or group. Take it in turns to see who can get the highest score by ringing the posts.

Alternatively devise your own game using kitchen roll holders and either circles of rope or rings of cardboard. Decide on a points scheme. Take aim!

TABLE BOULES

These can be used on a table top covered with a dark velvet curtain or something similar. The silver balls show up very well on a contrasting background.

When playing with VIPs, you can substitute the jack with a bigger ball that lights up or makes a noise.

 Thoughts for talks

Is our chief aim to score highly in life by being obedient to God?

In our attempt to get on in life do we knock others out of the way? "Love your neighbour as yourself." Mark 12:31

PRICKLY PILE-UP

With its little wooden porcupines, this has proved to be a popular game for individuals – others stopped what they were doing to watch.

Put 3 in a line on the table, as indicated, and see how many you can balance on these before any fall. Keep a record!

Thoughts for talks

Are we building our lives on a firm foundation? 1 Corinthians 3:10-15

How well balanced is our life? Are we weighed in the balance and found wanting?

COMMERCIAL SUPPLIERS

Amazon
Traditional Garden Games Garden
Quoits (£15)
Hoopla (£10)
Mini Boules (£4)
www.amazon.co.uk

Traditional Garden Games
Garden Quoits (£20)
12 Racecourse Road
East Ayton
Scarborough
YO13 9HP
www.traditionalgardengames.co.uk

Oxfam
Miniature Wooden Desk Skittles (£8)
www.oxfam.org.uk/shop

Great Little Trading Co
Prickly Pile-Up (£10)
Garden Quoits (£10)
Tel: 0844 848 6000
www.gltc.co.uk

House of Marbles
Prickly Pile-Up (£10)
Tel: 01626 835358
www.houseofmarbles.com

The Leprosy Mission
Desk Skittles (£10)
Tel: 0845 166 2253
www.tlmtrading.com

DESK SKITTLES

How to adapt game to make it easier to play

Cut a white card to fit on the base, making a hole for the pole. Mark the position of the skittles on the card, using a black pen.

To prevent skittles dropping onto the floor or the bed, place the skittles board on a high-edged tray.

HOW TO PLAY

Taking the ball in your fingers, let it go with a swing and see how many skittles you can knock down in one go.

Players take turns by swinging the ball once clockwise around behind the pole, the objective being to knock over all 9 skittles as the ball returns to the player. The ball must start its swing around the outside of the board so that it hits the skittles upon its return towards the player. 3 throws per turn are allowed and the skittles are only reset at the beginning of a turn or when all 9 have been knocked down.

**This game is especially good for those in bed!
Even if they have not got much manual dexterity,
they can have a go and VIPs love it.**

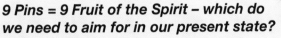

Thoughts for talks

9 Pins = 9 Fruit of the Spirit – which do we need to aim for in our present state?
Galations 5:22-23

DARTS AND TARGET BOARDS

There are a number of dartboard options available to buy that are suitable for people who are in bed or that can be adapted for the visually impaired (VIPs).

MAGNETIC DARTS

Hang or hold the dartboard a suitable distance away, bearing in mind you want the player to have an achievable goal and a fair rate of success. Holding the dartboard at a slight angle will help the darts to stick.

VIPs may need a little guidance.

DESKTOP DARTS

Good option for use in bed

People who are in bed can use the Desktop darts and board featured here, which you can put on their bedside table.

> ## Thoughts for talks
>
> *What is our aim in life? Caleb never lost sight of the goal!*
> See Numbers 14:6-9 and Deuteronomy 1:36
>
> *Are we like Him? How closely do we stick to following Jesus?*
> *Are we effective magnets or do we fall away quickly?*

VELCRO TARGET BOARD

Another good option for use in bed

Place a target board at a suitable distance away from the participant to get an achievable goal.

You can buy velcro target boards cheaply in many outlets.

'BAG A BIRD'

GUESS THE BAGGED BIRD

These toy birds all have their authentic calls and are available to buy from the RSPB.

They are a good investment as the game is very popular.

HOW TO PLAY

Place each bird in a different coloured bag or sock so it cannot be identified.

Gently squeeze the contents until you hear a sound. Which bird is it? Record your answer, noting the colour of the bag.

If you haven't a clue, have a guess!

Birds waiting to be guessed in their knitted socks

Holding the bagged birds and listening to the bird songs

'Bag a Bird'

What you need:

Something to hold the bird in, like bedsocks or cloth bags

Ribbon, or elastic bands to seal them in

Paper and pens

Thoughts for talks

How authentic are we? Could people tell we are Christian?

Give bedsocks away to those with the coldest feet!

13

BATON GAMES

PASS ON THE GOOD NEWS

Use lightweight foam sticks or cardboard tubes for batons. Hoops are made out of folded papers containing 'Good News' that are secured in the form of a circle.

Allocate 2 batons per table and 1 'Good News' hoop!

WHAT YOU NEED
See opposite page.

HOW TO PLAY

Players sit opposite each other in two rows, preferably at a table.

Putting a baton through the 'Good News' hoop, then putting the ends of their batons together, players can make a continuous path down which the news can pass.

Each player takes their turn to pass the Good News to the person sitting opposite them and then hands the baton to their immediate neighbour who then receives the Good News from the person across the table.

Continue until everyone has had a go and then send the Good News back again.

Thoughts for talks

With the first game it provides a talking point – we are meant to pass on the Good News of Jesus Christ – is it as easy as in the game?

'Passers-by' can pass on the Good News! *"Go into all the world and preach the good news to all creation."* Mark 16:15

PASS THE BALLOON

HOW TO PLAY

Each table needs 1 balloon and 4 batons.

One person holds the balloon between 2 batons and then passes it on to someone else, holding the other 2 batons.

Let everyone have a go and then reverse it.

Thoughts for talks

You could do some singing whilst the game is in progress!
'Speak to one another in psalms, hymns and spiritual songs...' Ephesians 5:19

CRACKERBACK

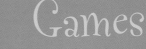

A fun game for VIPs that you can easily make.

HOW TO PLAY

The aim is to get your 'cracker' from one end of the table to the other and back in the shortest possible time. The two oranges provided are rolled at the cracker to move it forward. Each person takes a turn to roll an orange until the cracker reaches the end of the table.

The sound of the shaker inside the 'cracker' will let VIPs know where the object is.

When playing in teams, someone needs to time it.

COMMERCIAL SUPPLIERS

Baton Games
Swimming Noodles (2 for £8.50)
www.aqua-fun.co.uk

Crackerback

What you need:

Shaker from a toy shop

Wrapping paper

Sellotape

2 oranges

A long table (seats 6 people)

Make the cracker by covering the toy shaker with paper to make the required shape

Baton Games

What you need:

Lightweight foam sticks or cardboard tubes (like those in the centre of wrapping paper) or pipe lagging

Swimming Noodles can be cut in half to make batons!

Hoops made out of paper containing 'Good News' (eg a Bible verse or encouraging message)

Thoughts for talks

*Do we help each other along in life?
The body needs other members.*
1 Corinthians 12:27

PIT YOUR WITS

A good game for groups of people that can be adapted to suit many interests and abilities.

HOW TO MAKE
See opposite page.

HOW TO PLAY
Each player takes it in turn to take a card and reads out the subject. (Choose subjects that best suit your group).

The same player then flicks the spinner and reads out the letter it lands on.

The first person to call out an authentic answer beginning with that letter gets to keep the card.

The player with the most cards at the end of the game is the winner.

Texts from the Bible or other Bible topics can easily be included.

Spinner
Enlarge and colour in as required

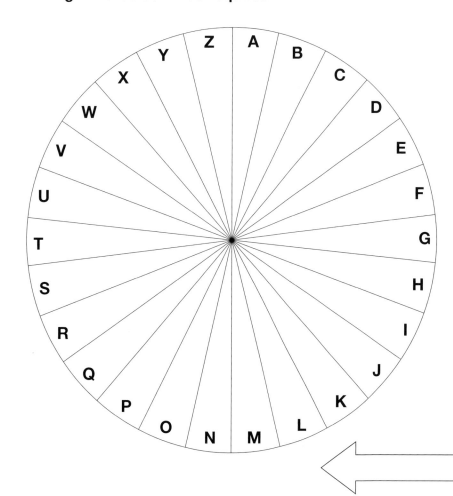

IDEAS FOR SUBJECTS FOR THE CARDS:

Girls or boys names

TV or Film stars

Historical characters

Biblical characters

Food or drink

Country or city names

Flowers

Vegetables

Animals

Football teams

Book titles

Books of the Bible

Sports

Songs

HOW TO PLAY

Gather together 20 items of different shapes, textures, and sizes and put them in a tub.

Pass round the items to each player and let them feel them all.

Then put everything back in the tub and cover over completely.

Record the items that players can remember – it's harder than you think!

HOW TO MAKE

Pit your Wits

1. Choose the subjects that best suit your group and stick the pictures and words onto different coloured cards.

2. Laminate for durability.

3. Make the Spinner by cutting a circle and arrow-pointer out of thick card and writing in the letters around the edge. Cover with transparent sticky-back plastic (eg Contact).

4. Use a paper fastener to secure them together.

Tip: Raising the Spinner base (eg by attaching Velcro pads to the base) allows the Spinner to rotate more freely.

Thoughts for talks

What does God want us to remember?
See Exodus 20:8 and Luke 22:19

What does God want us to forget?
See Isaiah 43:18 and Philippians 3:13

'FEELY' BOX AND 'GET IN SHAPE' BOARD

'FEELY' BOX
Christmas version

Find an old box and make a hole in it large enough to put your hand in and to accommodate the items to be used in this activity.

Cover the box in coloured paper and put the objects you are using inside. Shred some paper and put this in the box as loose filling.

What will you find?

WHAT YOU NEED
See opposite page.

HOW TO PLAY
Take it in turns to put one hand in the box and guess what they are – no peeking!

There are 7 different things to feel that are in some way connected to Christmas.

See if the person next to you can feel them and discuss how they may be related to the Christmas story.

In this Christmas version the following objects were used...

BELL
To tell the Good News of Jesus.
Acts 5:42

EGG
You must be born again.
John 3:3-7

CROSS
Jesus died on the Cross to save us from sin.
Col 2:13-15

CANDLE
Jesus said, "I am the light of the world."
John 8:12

CROWN
Jesus, born to be King.
John 18:37

GIFT
Jesus, the greatest Gift of all.
John 3:16

COW
Jesus was laid in a manger.
Luke 2:7

Use your own ideas for this and other times of year themes

'GET IN SHAPE' BOARD

Carefully cut out several different shapes from your polyboard with a craft knife. The shapes you cut out of the board become your puzzle pieces.

Paint the pieces in brightly coloured gloss and add small 'pulls' as handles to make the pieces easier to get out.

HOW TO PLAY
Try this blindfolded!

Take it in turns to put a shape in the right place. Can you guess just by feeling what they are?

At Christmas, for every piece successfully placed you can give the person a piece of a wooden nativity scene to be assembled as a joint project on the table.

'Feely' Box

What you need:
An old cardboard box

7 objects connected to a theme, eg Christmas or Easter

Shredded paper to fill the box

'Get in Shape' Board

What you need:
'Polyboard' from any art supplier – this is a lightweight foam board that can be cut easily with a craft knife and then painted

Plywood can be used as an alternative if you have a willing carpenter to cut the shapes out!

Thoughts for talks

Are we square pegs in round holes? Are we in the place God meant for us?

See Jeremiah 29:11
Are we shaping up to His plans for us?

MATCH-IT

This game can be used to celebrate the Christmas or Easter stories. Other sets can also be made on different themes.

HOW TO MAKE

1. Design sets of A4 cards, each with 4 different scenes and Bible verses (as illustrated).

2. Duplicate each A4 sheet, either by photocopying or printing, and laminate every sheet.

3. Take one A4 sheet from each set and cut out the 4 scenes. You now have a number of A4 cards, each with one set of 4 smaller cards which match the scenes on the A4 sheet.

HOW TO PLAY

Each player takes an A4 sheet.

The caller gathers up all the small cards. The caller then calls out the Bible verse on the card and the player with that verse on their sheet claims it. The one who completes their sheet first is the winner.

Small prizes can be given.

20

A useful tip

To ensure that one player does not complete their card long before everyone else, it is helpful to number the back of the smaller cards. The caller can then see at a glance if a particular player is too far ahead of the others.

In order to do this, take one set of cards before laminating and number each of the smaller cards on the back (the cards on one A4 sheet will have the number 1, the cards on another will have the number 2, etc).

COMMERCIAL SUPPLIERS

The clipart used to illustrate this game is obtainable from QuickArt CDs available from Authentic Media or at any Christian bookshop.

These images are copyright and may not be produced in any way unless the CDs are obtained.

Authentic Media
Tel: 0870 420 8188
(CDs £20 each)
www.authenticmedia.co.uk

CUBE TEMPLATE FOR WORD AND NUMBER GAMES

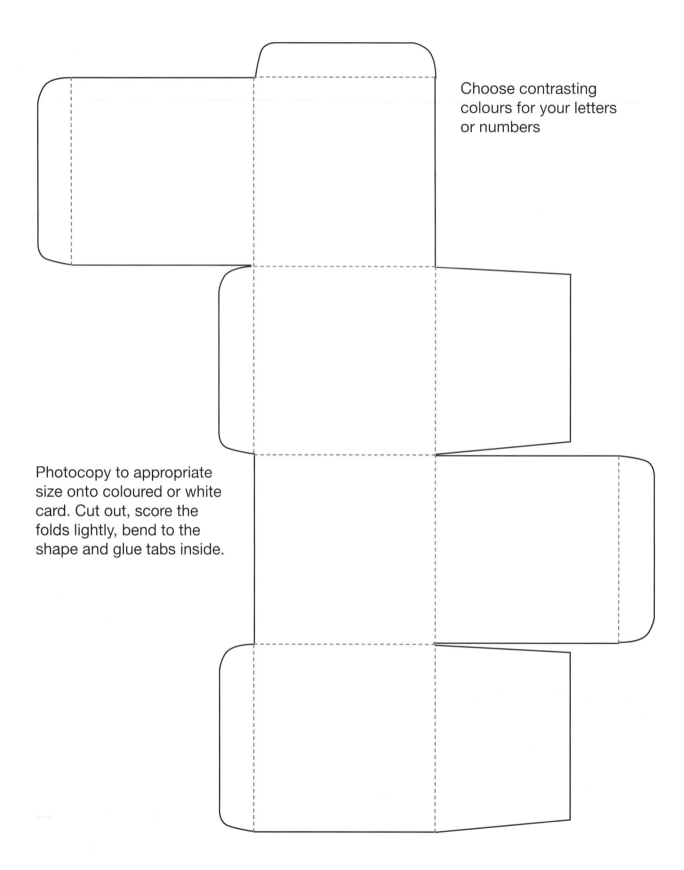

Choose contrasting colours for your letters or numbers

Photocopy to appropriate size onto coloured or white card. Cut out, score the folds lightly, bend to the shape and glue tabs inside.

Off-cuts of card can be inserted to make cubes more stable

LETTERS HAVE FUN

(Let us have fun!)

HOW TO MAKE

Giant Cube Letters
Make a cube from the template or use old boxes (a good way to recycle!).

Make at least five cubes.

Use contrasting colours.

Cut out random letters from fluorescent card (make sure you include several vowels).

Stick down on each face then cover with clear sticky-back plastic (eg Contact) before making into cubes.

GIANT CUBE WORD GAME

Cubes are accessible for people with little manual dexterity. They can be painted black or shaded with a giant felt pen to provide a good colour contrast. This game can be played by an individual or in groups.

HOW TO PLAY

1. Throw the cubes at random.

2. Make as many words as possible from the letters on the top face. You can time it and see who gets the most!

3. When that is done, take it in turns to throw again or turn the cubes over and use the next set of letters.

Thoughts for talks

You can choose words of spiritual resonance.
Choose a word relating to a theme (eg Christmas – incarnation; Easter – resurrection).

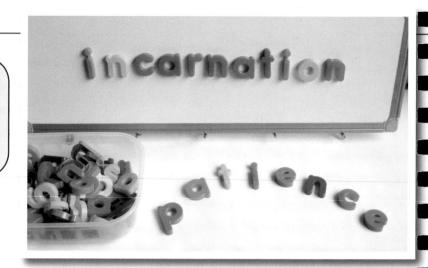

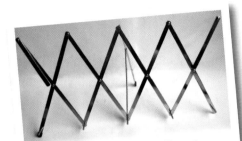

For those in bed providing a magnetic board with a support easel is a real help, ie a music stand like this could be used.

Make your own letters out of coloured card and stick pieces of magnetic ribbon on the back.

MAGNETIC WORD GAME

Use a magnetic board with large magnetic letters.

HOW TO PLAY

1. Put a long word on the magnetic board, eg SILENCE or INCARNATION.

2. Make as many 3-letter words as you can out of the word in 5 minutes. What is the longest word that you can get on your table from this word?

3. Letters may only be used once in a word.

WORD CHALLENGE

Ideal for VIPs. Stick on letters from fluorescent card and laminate for durability. (It is quite easy to make one's own large individual letters. Some colours like yellow and blue will be easier to identify).

NB. Extra large letters may be needed by some.

You will need to make a large pack of letter cards, 75 in total – as suggested below. There are six letter Es as this is the most common vowel, but only one letter Q as this is uncommon.

5A 2B 2C 4D 6E 3F 2G 2H 5I 1J 2K 2L 2M 3N 4O 3P 1Q 3R 3S 2T 5U 2V 2W 1X 2Y 1Z 3? 2&

HOW TO PLAY

1. Deal 8 cards to each player, which they can arrange facing up in front of them.

2. Lay 4 cards, with the letters facing up, in the centre.

3. Each player, in turn, uses at least one of the 4 central cards and as many of their own as they can use in forming one word.

4. After a player has made a word, all the letters used are placed on the bottom of the remaining pack. The central cards used are replenished from the remaining pack after each player has had their turn.

You could also play 'Snap' using either the letters or colours.

5. The winner is the first player to use up all their cards.

The ? card can be used as any letter the player requires, whether they are dealt one of these cards, or they are one of the central 4.

The & card is a bonus card which can be used as an 'A', 'N' or 'D', or any combination of these letters.

Players can work together to create words.

WORD FINDER CHALLENGE
HOW TO PLAY

1. Display a long word, eg PATIENCE.

2. Make as many different words as you can using any of the letters shown in 5 minutes.

3. Use letters only once.

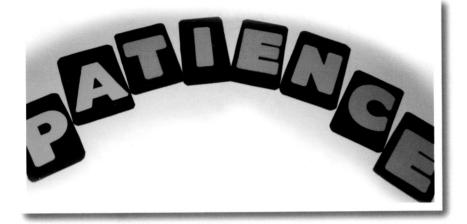

TRIPLETS
HOW TO PLAY

1. Make 3 rows of letters (as shown). Decide beforehand whether you are going to allow proper names and plurals.

2. Make as many words as you can with those letters that are in contact with each other. You can go vertically, horizontally and diagonally, but you must NOT jump letters!

HOW TO MAKE

Word Cards

Make the cards large and use very contrasting colours – eg white letters on black card or fluorescent as shown here.

Cut out each letter and stick down on the cards and then laminate.

For VIPs use felt or wooden letters so they are slightly raised. The letter can now be identified by touch.

COMMERCIAL SUPPLIERS

Early Learning Centre
Magnetic Letters & Numbers (£6)
Tel: 0871 231 3511
www.elc.co.uk

WHSmith
Magnetic Dry Wipe Board (£8)
Tel: 0870 444 6444
www.whsmith.co.uk

Ikea
Magnetic Board (£6)
www.ikea.com

Eg **PEA, PEAR, TRAP, SUPER, CUPS**

GIANT NUMBER GAMES

MAKE 50

This game can be played by individuals or in groups using either cubes or cards.

The cubes are ideal for those with less manual dexterity. A template for these cubes can be found on page 22.

HOW TO PLAY THE GAME USING CUBES

Place the four cubes on a table.

Using the numbers on the tops of the cubes only once, see how near to 50 you can get by adding, subtracting, multiplying, or dividing them together. The person getting nearest to 50 is the winner.

When finished, turn the cubes over to reveal the next four numbers to play again.

Either write the numbers clearly on white boxes or stick the numbers on so they can be clearly seen.

HOW TO PLAY THE GAME USING CARDS

Take the 18 black cards with the numbers 1-6 and sort into 3 piles. Shuffle each pile and place face up on the table.

Shuffle the 4th pile with the numbers 7-12 on it and place face up on the table.

The player who gets nearest to 50 by adding, subtracting, multiplying, or dividing the numbers on these cards takes the top cards off the pile to reveal the next four numbers.

The player with the most cards at the end of the game wins.

For a 'feely' version stick wooden or felt numbers on the cubes or cards.

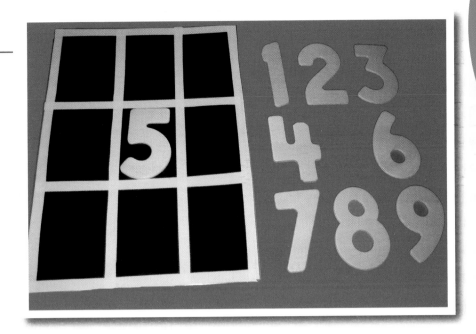

MAKE 15

Wooden numbers can easily be identified by touch which makes this a good game for the visually impaired. The game can be played by an individual or in groups.

HOW TO PLAY

Use the black board with 9 'squares' on it.

The player takes the numbers 1-9 and places them on the board so they add up to 15 all ways – ie across, vertically and diagonally.

The challenge is to see how quickly this can be done.

HOW TO MAKE

Make 50 Cubes

Make 4 cubes, three with numbers 1-6 and one with numbers 7-12. Write or stick the numbers on each face of the cubes.. Cover them with sticky-back plastic (eg Contact).

Make 50 Cards

Cut out eighteen 7 x 10 cm rectangles from black card.

Cut out six 8 x 10 cm rectangles from another piece of dark coloured card, eg blue (the larger size distinguishes the larger numbers).

On the black card stick 3 sets of numbers 1-6 cut out from a contrasting coloured card, eg yellow.

On the other coloured cards, stick 1 set of numbers 7-12, cut out from the same contrasting colour.

Laminate all 24 cards.

Make 15 Game

Make the board from a sheet of A4 black card.

Divide the card into 9 'squares' using white PVC tape.

Laminate the board for durability.

Use wooden or card numbers 1-9 which can be left plain or painted.

Thoughts for talks

1 - 1 way to God through Jesus – John 14:6 and Acts 4:12

2 - God made 2 great lights – Genesis 1:16 or 2 of every kind of animal – Genesis 6:19

3 - Father, Son and Holy Spirit

4 - The 4 Gospels – Matthew, Mark, Luke and John

5 - 5 loaves and 2 fish – God's provision – Mark 6:38

6 - Isaiah 6 – God's Glory, Holiness and Call

7 - 7 churches in Revelation – Revelation 1:4

8 - Only 8 were saved – Genesis 7:13

9 - 9 Fruit of the Spirit – Galatians 5:22-23

10 - The 10 Commandments – Exodus 20:3-17

11 - Jesus appeared to the Eleven – Mark 16:14

12 - The 12 tribes of Israel – Acts 26:7 or: The 12 disciples – Matthew 10:1

15 - I will add 15 years to your life – 2 Kings 20:6

50 - The Year of Jubilee – Leviticus 25:10

TANGRAM TEASER

This ancient Chinese puzzle is made up of a single square divided into 7 sections, as shown below. Re-arrange the pieces to make hundreds of designs!

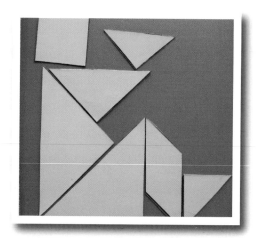

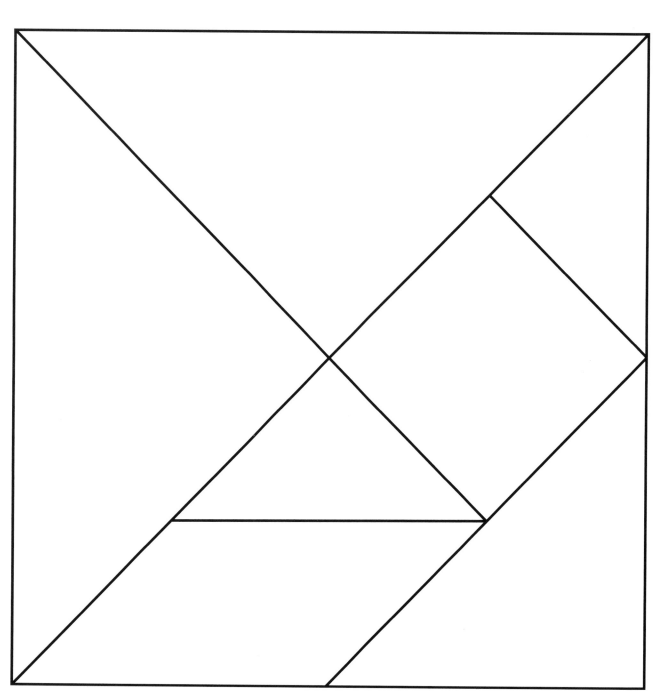

HOW TO MAKE

Tangrams

Photocopy the square shown on page 28, at the size required onto coloured card.

(You may want to keep a copy of the intact square, as it is not as easy as it looks to remake!)

Cut out the 7 shapes as accurately as possible (after laminating), and try to make some interesting shapes of your own.

There are over 300 different designs* you can make with the pieces, including numbers 1-9 and all the letters of the alphabet, as well as people and creatures!

This can either be a group activity or done individually.

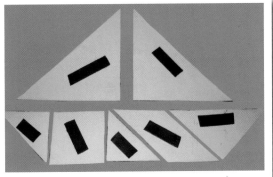

For those who are bedridden – laminate the pieces, then using strong glue (eg UHU) attach strips of magnetic tape as shown in the picture and provide a magnetic board (bits dropping in the sheets can be a nightmare).

* A useful resource for ideas is the book '300 Tangrams: The Ancient Shapes Game' by Lagoon Books

Thoughts for talks

God can make something new from the broken pieces of our lives if we give them to Him! See Jeremiah 29:11 and 2 Corinthians 5:17

5 PIECE CROSS

TEMPLATE

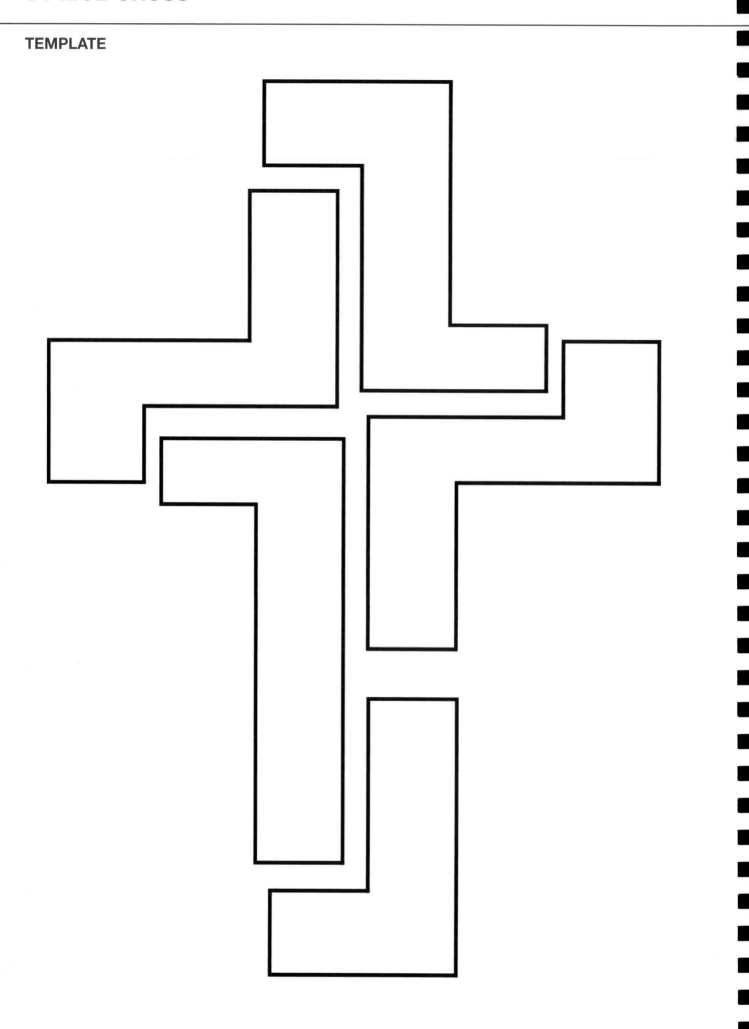

HOW TO MAKE

Using the template on page 30, photocopy the shapes onto coloured or white card. Laminate and then cut out the individual pieces.

See who can make the cross first.

Affix magnetic tape to the pieces to hold the positions and provide a magnetic board for people in bed.

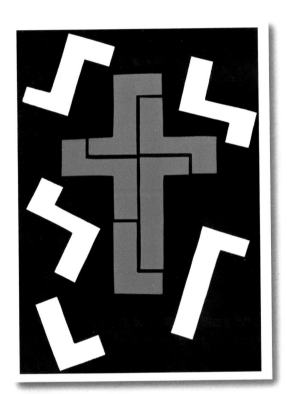

COMMERCIAL SUPPLIERS

Staples
Aluminium frame combo board (£15)
www.staples.co.uk

Ikea
Magnetic Board (£6)
www.ikea.com

Thoughts for talks

See 1 Corinthians 11:24 – **'and when he had given thanks, he broke it and said, "This is my body, which is for you; do this in remembrance of me."**

TEMPLATE

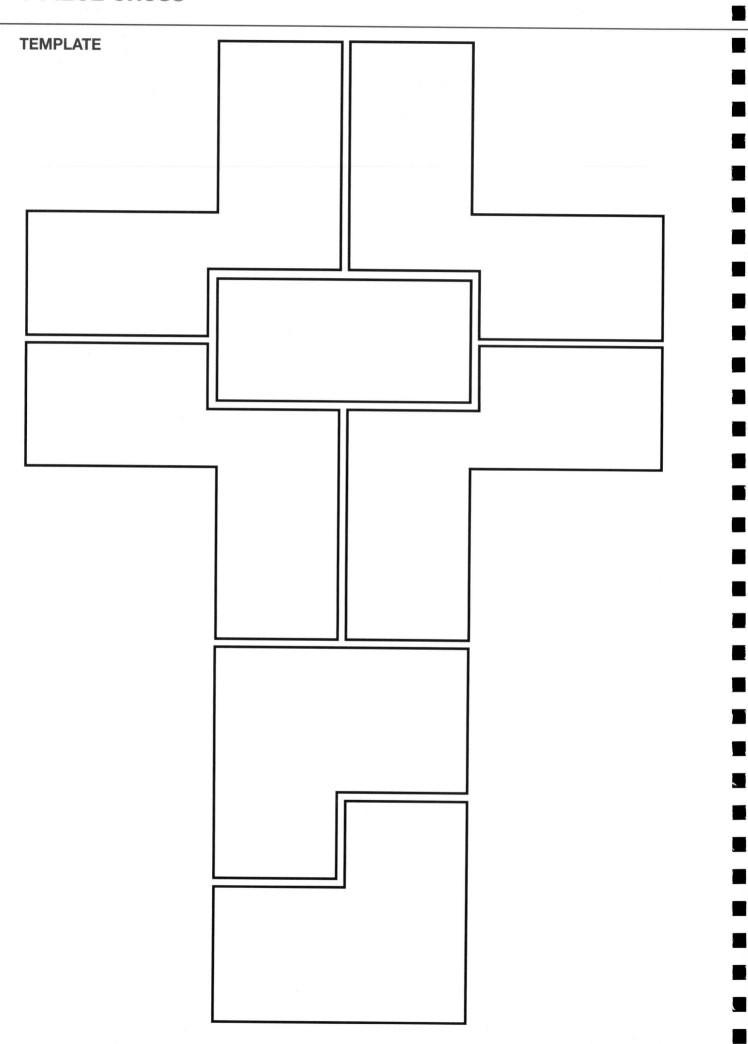

HOW TO MAKE

1. Photocopy template opposite onto paper or card.

2. Clearly write an appropriate Bible verse using all the 7 pieces that will make up the cross.

3. Make as many photocopies of this as you need.

4. Laminate if required, then cut out the pieces.

What you need:

Paper or card (coloured if desired)

Scissors

Laminator and pouches (optional)

HOW TO PLAY

Arrange the shapes to form the cross so that you can also read the Bible verse.

Time yourselves.

Now can you cover it up and remember the Bible verse?

Blessed are | those who

JESUS DIED FOR
_____

have not | seen and

yet have believed.

John 20:29

Side showing Bible verse – put your own verse on!

Use other texts for different themes.

Can you put your name in the central section?

JOINTED MAN

ASSEMBLE AS FOLLOWS:

1. Place right upper arm behind neck, place body on top of neck and on that left upper arm. Secure all 4 pieces with a paper fastener.

2. At bottom of body place right thigh underneath and left thigh on top. Secure with paper fastener.

3. Add forearm to each upper arm and lower leg to each thigh and fasten as before.

4. Add foot to each lower leg and secure with paper fasteners.

5. Ensure all parts can be moved to desired position.

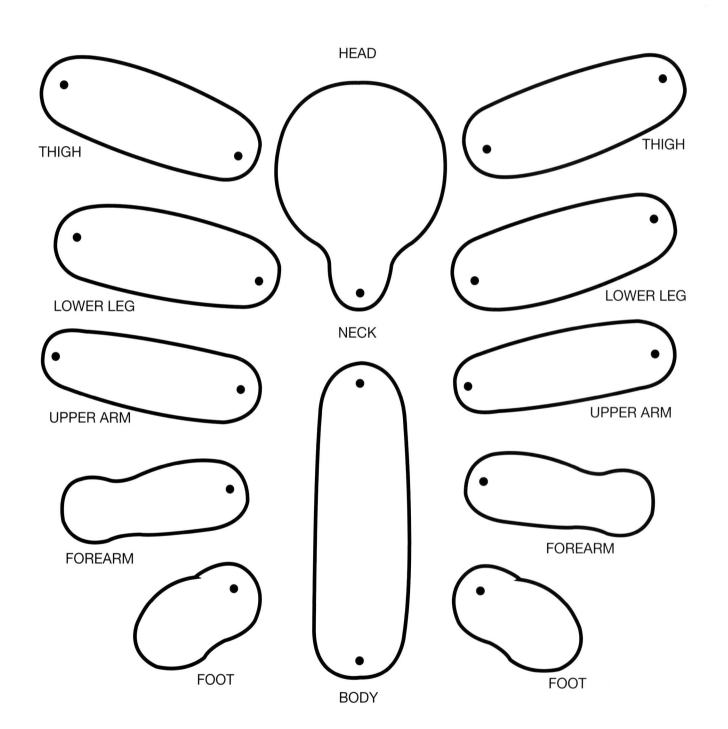

SUGGESTIONS FOR USE

You can use the Jointed Man:

- to illustrate 1 Corinthians 12 – one body, many parts.
- in a Bible story, to convey the action of one or more characters.
- to imagine what your response to different situations would be.

HOW TO MAKE

This is easy to make out of cardboard/thin card.

Simply enlarge the pieces to the required size – paste onto coloured cardboard or paint it and cut out and assemble using split pins.

It is useful to have different colours for front and back – whatever shows up best on your background can be used.

Thoughts for talks

Is it our attitude of heart or position of the body that counts most when it comes to worship? Who was 'out of joint' for us?
See Psalm 22, especially verse 14.

MARBLING

Easy to do, with a minimum of effort and great results.

This creative activity is especially good for those in bed or with limited mobility. These colourful creations can also be done by the visually impaired.

People are very excited by the marbling process and you can never predict how the finished item will look. Those who normally have no opportunity to do something so creative are thrilled at what they can produce.

There are two types of marbling listed on the following pages – Marabu and Pebeo. They each have different uses, different materials and require different techniques.

Decorated eggs using Marabu ink

Thoughts for talks *Each item is unique. It is very satisfying as our great Creator has made us in His image but totally unique.*

Marbling with eggcellent results!

Some personal experiences

*Ernest** had a severe stroke, which left him unable to communicate well and **with little mobility, except in one hand**. However, he was game to have a go and the resultant marbled egg, which he did with close supervision, was very beautiful – when his wife came in later she could not believe he had done it and, of course, we let her do one.

It is not difficult to master marbling

Another lady, with one arm in plaster, had a go and was **thrilled with the result**. Yet another, very confused individual had great joy when her egg turned out so well. She particularly appreciated it because I later found out that she used to be something of a painter herself.

In the reception area of the Home I watched *Lucy** emerge from her mother's room and she seemed very down. On enquiring what was the matter she told me that her mum was far from well and extremely low. Having brought only a few eggs in with me that morning I now had only one left and had been wondering who best to use it with. I asked her if she had a few more minutes to spare and she agreed to come back to her mother's room with me.

Her mother lay dejectedly, in her special chair, but was willing to see what would happen to the egg when she followed what I told her to do. The result was one of the best marbled eggs I have ever seen and the effect on both mother and daughter was amazing. Mum came alive!

As a consequence, when the daughter left later on, it was on a high note and I thanked God for a creative pastime, done so easily, that had given such relief.

*Not their real names

MARBLING (PEBEO)

MARBLING INSTRUCTIONS FOR USE WITH PEBEO INKS
For marbling paper or thin card

Activities

Marbling
Pebeo inks for
paper or card

HOW TO MARBLE

- Make up the thickener solution as instructed on the bottle **two hours before you start**. Pour a 2-3 cm layer of the mixture into a plastic tray and leave to stand.
- Identify each item to be marbled by writing the person's name on it in pencil.
- Drop 5 or 6 drops of each colour required onto the surface of the mixture and allow to spread for a few seconds.
- Gently swirl a pattern on the surface of the mixture, using a plastic fork or a cocktail stick **(fig A)**.
- Carefully lay the item you want to marble on the surface of the mixture, flattening any curled edges (the paper should not be completely immersed).
- Leave for 10-15 seconds before lifting it out **(fig B)**. Let surplus colour drip off, then over a washing-up bowl rinse with water to remove excess paint.
- Allow to dry flat – spread on newspaper.
- You can then mount the work on card, perhaps adding an appropriate Bible verse, and laminate.

Note: As the solution gets dirtier, just continue to use fresh paint – it still works.

Pebeo marbling

COMMERCIAL SUPPLIERS

Blots Pens
Pebeo Marbling Initiation Kit: Set includes bath thickener and five bottles of marbling inks – White, Lemon Yellow, Vermillion, Emerald, Cyan (£17.50)
Individual colours available (£3.50)
www.blotspens.co.uk

Marbling (Pebeo inks)
What you need:

- Shallow plastic tray (larger than the item to be marbled)
- Pebeo marbling thickener
- Pebeo marbling colours
- Plastic forks
- Plain paper rectangles or other shapes
- Assorted coloured card or paper
- Laminator and pouches (optional)
- Roll of paper towel
- Jug of water
- Washing up bowl
- Newspapers
- Hairdryer (optional)
- Helpers (one for every 3-4 people) who are fully conversant with marbling procedures

Thoughts for talks

As the marbling solution gets more 'yucky' you can ask whether the participant thinks anything beautiful can come from it. Then as you wash surplus paint it is, where appropriate, good to point out that God cleanses us if we come to Him and is able to bring out the best in us.

"Therefore if anyone is in Christ he is a new creation; the old has gone, the new has come!" 2 Corinthians 5 v 17

MARBLING (MARABU)

MARBLING INSTRUCTIONS FOR USE WITH MARABU INKS
(using the 'dipping' technique)
For marbling: Small boxes, Plastic eggs, Bookmarks, Photo frames

HOW TO MARBLE

Fill marbling container (large yoghurt pot) with cold water to approx 2cms from the top (make sure the container is big enough for object to be completely submerged in the water).

Let 2 or 3 drops of different coloured inks fall onto the surface of the water **(fig A)**. Swirl the paint immediately, using the tip of a cocktail stick to create patterns **(figs B & C)**.

Please note: The above process needs to be repeated for each item that is to be marbled. Any remaining ink from your previous marbling needs to be 'cleared' from the container using a length of thin card **(fig D)**. (This can be used to make a bookmark – see right).

Now decide what you want to marble.

Marbled Eggs:

Insert the pointed end of a kebab stick into the egg and write the person's name on a narrow adhesive label half-way down the stick.

Dip the egg slowly into the coloured water, making sure there is a continual push down **(fig E)**. (If you stop before it is completely submerged you will get an unsightly ring around the egg). Then take out the egg quickly **(fig F)**.

Shake off surplus water and leave eggs to dry on their sticks in a container of sand (about 10 minutes).

Tips: We found that, for some reason, certain yoghurt pots did not work, as the paint clung to the cocktail sticks when they were used to make the pattern – so try it yourself first.

There is a template for a box in which to place a marbled egg on page 40. This too can be decorated.

MARBLING

Marbled Bookmarks:

This is an ideal way of 'clearing' ink after marbling other items – see note on page 38.

Cut up strips of card and label one end with the person's name.

At this end of the card, either punch a hole or attach a paperclip.

Then, holding the same end of the card, quickly submerge as much of the card as possible without getting paint on your fingers or the person's name, and remove quickly.

Hang up to dry by putting a length of string through the hole you punched beforehand, or threading string through the paper clip. (A hairdryer can speed up the drying process).

Once dried, trim the end of the card.

Finish the bookmark by sticking it to coloured card if one side has not come out well. Any blank patches can be filled in with coloured pencils, or by adding small pictures or Bible verses. Laminate and cut out.

Marbled Gift Boxes:

Make up the box from the instructions on page 42.

Label with owner's name inside both the lid and bottom.

Lower the box lid or bottom to just below the surface of the water after dropping the colours in, using gentle pressure from either your fingers or tweezers inside the centre of the box.

Pull out quickly using tweezers and place on a small upturned yoghurt pot to dry.

COMMERCIAL SUPPLIERS

Time to Sow
Marabu - Easy Marble Marbling Ink: Set includes six jars of marble paint – Yellow, Red, Blue, Green, Black, White (£12)
Individual colours available (£3)
White Plastic Eggs (10 for £1.25, 50 for £5)
Tel: 01462 639829
www.timetosow.com

Marbling (Marabu)
What you need:

- Waterproof tablecloth or newspapers
- Marabu marbling inks
- Disposable gloves
- Kitchen towel
- Large and small yoghurt pots and water
- Small boxes made from template on page 42
- Plastic eggs
- Assorted paper and card
- Kebab and cocktail sticks
- Pencils
- Narrow adhesive labels
- Hairdryer
- Scissors
- Hole punch or paper clips and string
- Heavy container containing sand
- Tweezers
- Sellotape
- Glue
- Laminator and pouches (optional)
- Helpers (one for every 3-4 people) who are fully conversant with marbling procedures

Thoughts for talks *Our great Creator God has put within each person a love of making things and often in people's older years they seldom have the chance to make anything beautiful.*

I believe that is why so many find marbling deeply satisfying. Furthermore it is an achievable goal – when the ravages of old age render fingers unable to knit, sew, etc.

BOX TEMPLATE

This simple box template can be photocopied and stuck onto card. It is then easy to decorate, cut out and make.

This makes a good gift box for marbled eggs (see page 38).

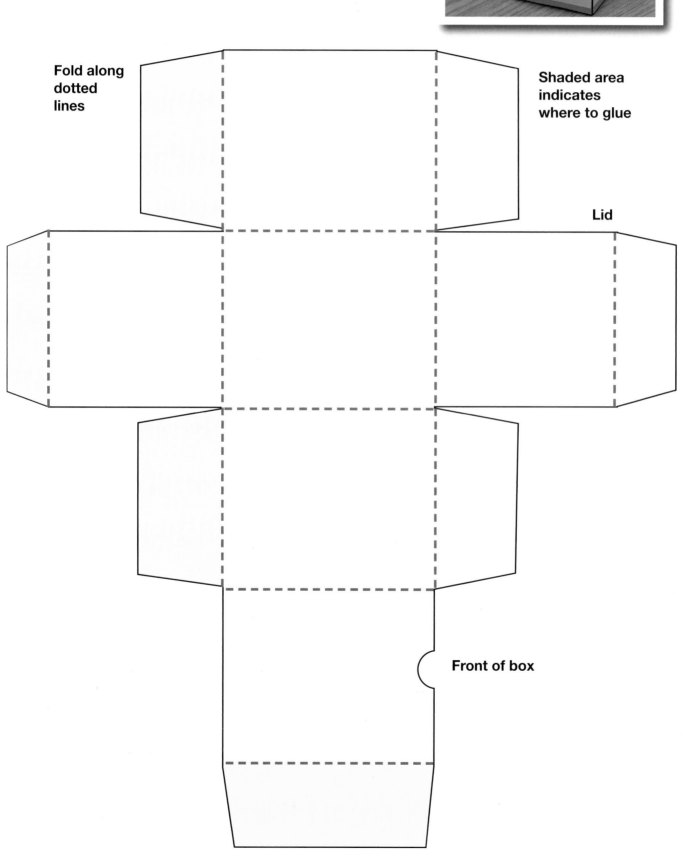

Fold along dotted lines

Shaded area indicates where to glue

Lid

Front of box

Eggcellent gift ideas!

Egg Decorations

I was able to purchase coloured plastic eggs at Poundland which were hinged in the middle, allowing you to open them and insert small gifts, such as a few chocolates (at Easter, small chocolate eggs with chick and an Easter Bible verse). For diabetics substitute the chocolate with seedless grapes.

The eggs had a small hole at both ends, so I put a piece of Blu-tack inside one of the sections to block the hole, firmly closed the egg and used a cocktail stick through the other hole to hold it for dipping.

The results were just as good as with the plain white eggs.

When dry, these eggs can be stood on bottle caps, secured with Blu-tack. They can also be suspended from twigs to make an Easter tree.

Marbled Photo Frames

Photo frames made out of card can also be marbled.

COMMERCIAL SUPPLIERS
Baker Ross
Photo frames
Pack of 12 (£4)
www.bakerross.co.uk

"He is not here; for He is risen."

Matthew 28 v 6

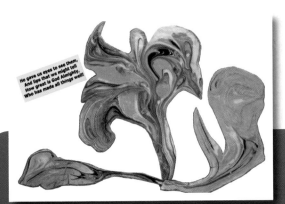

He gave us eyes to see them,
And lips that we might tell
How great is God Almighty,
Who has made all things well!

When the dove returned to him...
Noah knew the water had receded from the earth.
Genesis 8:11

Some personal experiences

A lady who was 102 years old and confined to bed had great joy in producing a marbled egg.

The lady in the next room was less well disposed to trying anything new. When she came into the Home, she felt there was no life to be had now that she was in her 90's.

I had the greatest difficulty in coaxing her to try out marbling. In the end, however, she agreed to join in. The resultant butterfly was a stunning creation which had her and her subsequent visitors amazed – especially when she explained that a certain persistent lady had not given her a paintbrush but a plastic fork with which to make the pattern!

Her 'masterpiece' has pride of place on the side of the cupboard, near her chair, with a little rhyme that encourages her to try new things and ask God for His help.

The next time I arrived at the Home with a variety of things, she was intrigued and there was no difficulty in getting her to have a go – in fact she produced two beautiful eggs. They both turned out very different and she was thrilled with them.

HOW TO MAKE A GLUELESS BOX

Although this box looks complicated for older people to make, it's easier once they watch you do it.

Both the base and the lid are made in exactly the same way. Follow steps 1-9 for the base and then repeat steps 1-9 for the lid.

1. Measure out a 15cm square and a 14cm square on a sheet of A4 thin card. Draw in diagonal lines from corner to corner and carefully cut out the squares. **(fig A)**

2. With one square laying out on the table like a diamond, fold each corner in to the centre. **(fig B)**

3. Create another crease by folding each corner out from the centre to the folded edge **(fig C)**. Open out flat.

4. Take the corner nearest you and fold it away from you, past the centre, to the second crease down on the opposite side. Unfold and repeat for each corner. **(fig D)**

5. Open out flat. The small square in the centre, created by creases, will form the base of your box. **(fig E)**

6. Make four cuts, from the first fold to the third fold (along the solid red lines). **(fig F)**

7. Fold the corners of the larger triangles into the centre and raise the sides up. **(fig G)**

8. Take the two wings and fold towards each other to make the third side of the box. Repeat for the other wings to construct fourth side. **(fig H)**

9. Take the corner of the small triangle and fold over the wings and down to the centre of the base of the box. Tuck the corners in and press all around to secure the box. **(fig J)**

Check out the support page
www.lcm.org.uk/funwithapurpose
for extra tips and updates.

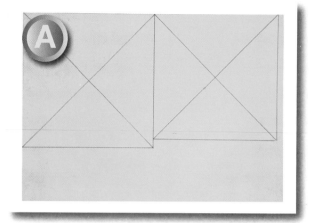

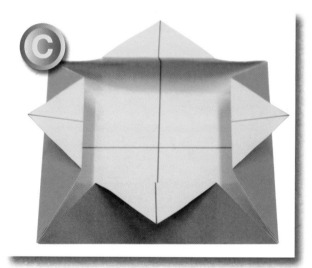

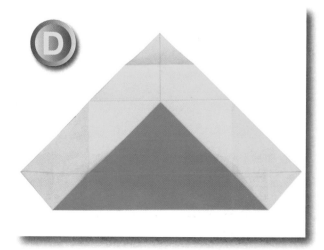

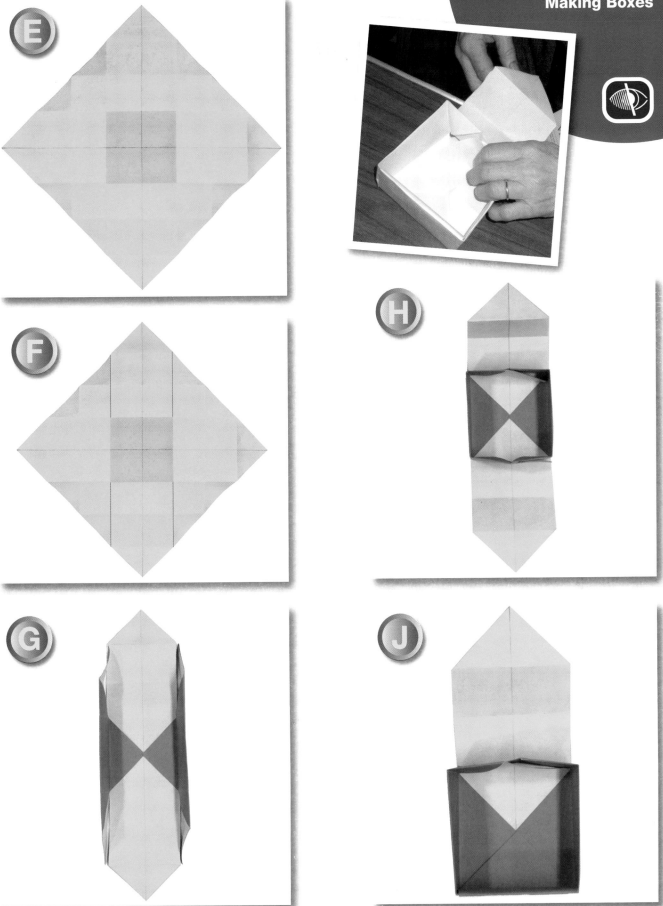

E

F

G

H

J

You can make boxes of different sizes (eg 12cm square for a base and 13cm square for the lid) and that box should fit inside the one you have just made. Decorate in a variety of ways – marbling, self-adhesive stickers, tiny rolls of tissue paper, crayonings, etc, or make from old Christmas or birthday cards with the picture to show on the outside!

STENCILS

This is very useful for those with less able fingers or for the visually impaired and usually gives amazing results which are very satisfying for the person involved.

Choose simple designs, perhaps relating to a theme that has been chosen, and secure well to the paper background by means of paper clips.

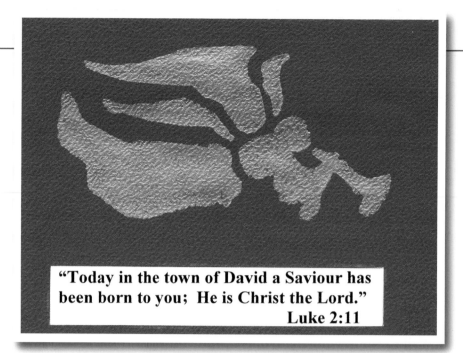

"Today in the town of David a Saviour has been born to you; He is Christ the Lord."
Luke 2:11

HOW TO MAKE

Using blow pens, felt tip pens, large crayons, pencils or paint, fill up the outline provided by the stencil.

If using paint try not to use any water with it but straight from the paint pot. Let dry before carefully removing the stencil from the paper. Outline with a black pen if people have gone slightly over the edges. Add an appropriate Bible verse if desired – having mounted their stencilling on a contrasting background (do put their name on the back!) – and laminate. Wipe the stencil clean, ready for the next user.

The stencils can be used to illustrate Bible verses or poems such as 'The Rose' on page 56

2 Corinthians 5:17

'If anyone is in Christ he is a new creation.'

44

MELTING BEADS

It is best to use giant size hama beads as the normal hama beads can be too small for some older people to handle.

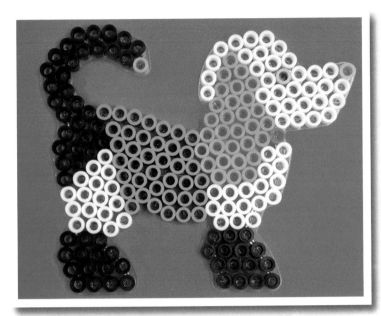

Make your pattern by placing the beads onto the pegs on the pegboard, which can be used again and again.

Lay ironing paper provided (greaseproof paper will do) over the beads and iron – as the pattern begins to show through the paper the beads will cohere together.

To make the project more durable, iron the bottom side as well. (Don't forget to use ironing paper!)

Let your project cool off before popping it off the pegboard – 3-4 mins minimum.

Finished projects can be used as coasters, table mats or simple decorations.

COMMERCIAL SUPPLIERS

Mail Order Express
My First Maxi Hama Beads:
Variety of sets and shapes (£3.50+)
Tel: 0871 222 1500
www.mailorderexpress.com

Dream Crafts
Melty Beads Book (£8)
Tel: 020 8873 2893
www.dreamcraftstore.co.uk

Amazon
Giant gift box (£12.95)
www.amazon.co.uk

Early Learning Centre
Ten pots of poster paint
and paintbrush (£4)
www.elc.co.uk

Thoughts for talks

*Do we let God's word melt our hearts
so that His design shows up?*
'He sends his word and melts them.' Psalm 147:18

BELLEPLATE MUSIC

It's amazing what can be done with aluminium!

Sylvena's experiences with Belleplates - affordable, lightweight alternatives to handbells for tune ringing.

These are wonderful for building 'community' and our God is a God of community. For our Care Home residents the music provided needed adapting so that large bold-type letters (font 26) and the appropriate words (font 24) written directly underneath were typed out and all the notes were colour coded.

I found that it was helpful to put the correct syllable of each word directly below the correct note. Having done this, to help with the timing, we always sing the words.

This has been great as those who for some reason are not happy handling a bell can still join in.

One completely blind gentleman who had been a musician knew exactly where to come in although he could not see the music. Other blind people find it more difficult but if they have any sense of rhythm they can join in using a triangle or tambourine.

The first song we ever did and that we always start with is 'Old MacDonald had a farm' and I discovered that a few hand puppets livened things up – in particular a cawing crow. On the farm he had some crows! – with a caw, caw here and a caw, caw there.

No matter it was a fluorescent purple crow, one blind lady got very adept at handling it – to the great delight of us all.

You can also use your favourite hymns and choruses in addition to using the songs in the pack.

JESUS LOVES ME.

G E E D   E G G   A A C' A   A G G
Jesus loves me, this I know, tho' my hair is white as snow.

G E E   D E G G   A A G C   E D C
Tho' my sight is growing dim, Still He bids me trust in Him.

G E G A C'   G E C ED
Yes, Jesus loves me   Yes, Jesus loves me

Chorus

G E G A C'   A G C E D C
Yes, Jesus loves me   the   Bible tells me so.

G E E   D E G G   A AC' A A G G
Tho' my steps are oh, so slow, With my hand in His I'll go.

G E   E D E G G   A A G C E D C
On thro' life, let come what may, He'll be there to lead the
                                                            way.

Chorus.

G   E E D E G G   A A   C' A   A G G
Tho' I am no longer young, I have much which He's begun.

G E   E   D   E G G   A A G C E D C
Let me serve Christ with a smile, Go with others the extra
                                                            mile.

Chorus.

An example of how one old chorus has been adapted for seniors

Thoughts for talks

One of the reasons to use them
– *see Colossians 3:16*

PARACHUTES

Gentle exercise for the elderly and those in wheelchairs.

If you can't get a Parachute, an alternative would be a sheet or large tablecloth. Use a sponge ball, a musical ball or an inflatable beach ball.

It can be great fun, using the chute from a sitting position, to lob a sponge ball or musical ball over the heads of players holding the chute on the opposite edge.

'Trap' a mobile person who tries to get from one side of the chute to the other whilst they raise it in the air and then bring it down quickly.

Create waves to music.

COMMERCIAL SUPPLIERS

BELLEPLATES
Belleplates
Sets of Belleplates
and instructions (from £362)
Music (£2+)
Tel: 01784 255961
www.belleplates.com

PARACHUTES
Early Learning Centre
Parachute (£15)
Tel: 0871 231 3511
www.elc.co.uk

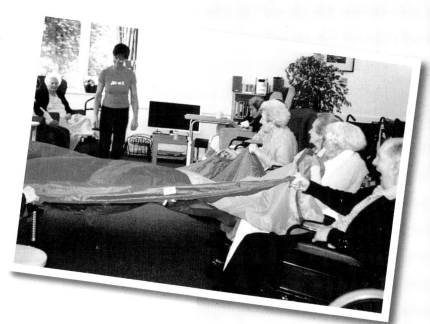

Are we unstable in all we do - blown and tossed about by the wind?

Thoughts for talks

*Can we say with the Psalmist:
"I have trusted in the Lord without wavering."?*
See Psalm 26:1; James 1:6-8

DVD LIBRARY

Use of a portable DVD player for Care Home, hospital and home visits

For people in Care Homes, DVDs can be an 'oasis in the desert' as many cannot even leave their rooms.

There may be nothing on TV that they want to watch and, if it is at the other side of the room, they may not be able to see it clearly; but a portable DVD player on their 'over the bed' table can be of great benefit.

There are some wonderful Christian DVDs now of varying lengths. 'Gift of Hope' was one DVD that had a profound effect on three residents who had 'given up' on life and lost all hope.

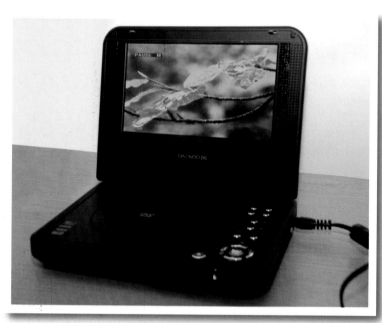

One viewer described the ones shown as "so relaxing".

"The water seems almost to splash out from the screen and it is as if we were there!", he said.

Similar sentiments were voiced by others.

It also helps them forget their pain. Another lady with dementia (concentration span about 5 minutes) was extremely restless and could not seem to settle. She agreed to watch 'Celtic Wonders of Creation' and was totally glued to the screen for the whole duration of the film (about 45 minutes). I was astonished as she constantly referred delightedly to either the music and/or the scenery throughout its showing. She too was also helped and went from restlessness to calm.

Doubtful about the use of such a resource in a hospital setting, at the suggestion of my gap year volunteer I reluctantly took along the DVD player and a 20-minute DVD 'Touch of the Master's Hand' to the hospital.

The lady we had gone to visit was in her nineties and had had a very bad day. She was almost bored to tears. Watching this film 'made her day', she said, and months later she could vividly remember what she had seen!

In the Nursing Home some residents were soon confident enough to operate the player themselves and would watch the film two or three times before I got back to them. Others needed me to stay with them, for a variety of reasons.

Lively discussions often took place as a consequence of seeing and hearing these things and many questions were asked.

Church groups visiting Care Homes on a regular basis could perhaps build up a collection of DVDs to take in.

Some of Sylvena's favourite DVDs

Gift of Hope: The Tony Melendez Story

A man with no arms plays guitar with his feet. Challenges us to embrace life. *45mins*

A lady who wasn't eating or drinking and seemed to want to die watched this and was soon seen back in the lounge.

© Vision Videos

£12.50   www.trinityvision.co.uk

Reflections on Psalm 23

For people with cancer and other terminal conditions. *Thirteen 8-minute programmes*

Beautiful photography – really made a difference to a lady whose sister had just been diagnosed with cancer.

©. Vision Videos

£6   www.veriteshop.co.uk

Celtic Wonders of Creation

Marvellous photography and beautiful music. *46mins*

© Authentic Media

£10   www.eden.co.uk

Touch of the Master's Hand

Uses the story of a violin to get its powerful message home. *20mins*

© Visual Transit Authority

Distributed by Vision Video

£12.50   www.trinityvision.co.uk

Footprints in the sand

Stunning views and linked with the famous poem.

After several residents had watched this the lady in charge asked for details of the book that tells the story of the poem so she could read it with them.

© Classic Fox Records (also through Leprosy Mission)

£8   www.namesakes.co.uk

The Tanglewoods' Secret

Based on the book by Patricia St John

Treasures of the Snow

Based on the book by Patricia St John

Both of these films have captivated the elderly people who were going through hard times.

© International Films

£13   www.amazon.co.uk

Living Faith

The life story of Julie Sheldon and reflections on Living Water.

Another gripping testimony that made compulsive viewing for some.

Supplied by Evangelical Films

£10   www.nationwidechristiantrust.com

A Billy Graham Music Homecoming – Vols 1 and 2.

A musical treat and folk were impressed, not just by that but by the faces of all the participants. A lady undergoing chemotherapy found this a continual means of encouragement and relaxation.

© Spring House Inc. (Distributed in Europe by Alliance Music)

£12.50   www.christianbits.co.uk

Lee Abbey Reflections

Inspirational music, scenery and images.

A lady was finding life very tough – her home of 77 years put on the market – she watched this three times and it ministered to her needs that afternoon and helped her through subsequent days.

© Active Media Publishing Ltd

£19   www.christianbits.co.uk

It's a Boy

Puts over the nativity story in a different way. *29mins*

Even residents who had signified they were not interested in this were drawn into seeing this hilarious tale. However, it is not just humorous but makes a point.

© Breakout Trust

£9   www.christianbits.co.uk

Amazing Grace

Gaither Gospel Series – a very popular series

Lifted the flagging spirits of several elderly people.

© Spring House Inc (Distributed in Europe by Authentic Media)

£15   www.gospelwithintegrity.com

LIFE STORY PROJECT

HOW TO COMPILE A LIFE STORY

People can find great pleasure and fulfilment in creating their own life story. This can be done using a 'Story of my life' ring-binder, picture scrapbook and a personal treasure box. VIPs may find it helpful to record their life story on an MP3 player, etc.

Relatives and carers can be a good resource and usually enjoy being involved.

You could cover each of the following areas, listing the information and then providing special thoughts on each topic when they come to mind:

- Growing up – birthdate, birthplace, childhood, school/university, teachers, friendships

- Work – first job, career, other jobs such as housekeeping

- Marriage – courtship, wedding, honeymoon

- Home – garden, neighbours, pets

- Family – parents, children, grandchildren, great-grandchildren

- Faith – favourite hymn, church, religion, community

- Hobbies – pastimes past and present

- Favourites – food and drink, sayings/proverbs, holiday destinations, special memories

- Other subjects – dress, fashion, work clothes down the years, War years, comedy now and then, certificates

Bring up to date – birthdays, dominant memories

Check out the support page
www.lcm.org.uk/funwithapurpose
for extra tips and updates.

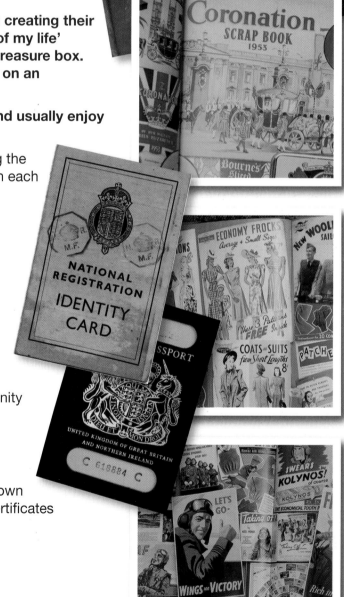

The daughter of a resident of a nursing home shares her experience of creating a 'Life Story' project with her father.

"I was given an outline of a life story project to use with my father, George, who is a resident of a Bromley Nursing Home. He has Parkinson's disease with a significant degree of cognitive impairment. His short- and long-term memory is declining rapidly and it was suggested that I use this resource while he was still able to recall something of his past.

Over several months, I talked through the different sections with my father, making rough notes as he remembered incidents from the past. It took some time, as he was often too tired or too confused, but we had many enjoyable and sometimes quite revealing and emotional sessions as he recalled his childhood and working life.

At the same time, I began a long overdue sort through my father's papers and photographs, and these documents and pictures provided a focus for discussion and helped to jog his memory. This also enabled me to check dates and facts and clarify some of the anecdotal information he had given me.

I read each section to him once I had written it up, and his first response was, "How do you know all this?" We now regularly read his book together and it continues to be something that he enjoys and helps him to hold on to his rapidly weakening memory.

I have shown the book to my daughters who now know a great deal more about their granddad than they did before. It's also good for some family members who find it hard to know what to chat to George about; for them it provides a focus for conversation and makes visits easier. The book also shows that, while George may be in need of care and being washed and dressed, he is also an interesting and intelligent man who has dedicated his life to helping others.

This is a project which has enthused a number of my friends who have elderly parents themselves – those who have seen Dad's book have now been inspired to do something similar with their own parents."

Clare (daughter)

RESOURCES

A helpful DVD entitled 'Talking is caring' is available from Help in Sight Training (£25).
Tel. 01227 752199

It highlights the importance of making a connection with older people through conversation and sharing memories.

Help in Sight Training also run workshops for care workers to introduce them to Life Story Project work and have various conversation-generating tools.

COMMERCIAL SUPPLIERS

The Wartime Scrapbook featured on this page together with other helpful books in this series are available from **www.amazon.co.uk** (£13).

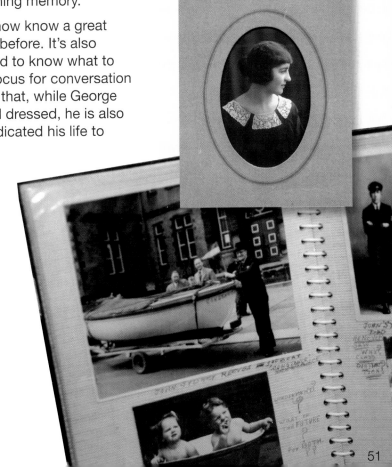

EVANGECUBE

This unique box puzzle has been developed in the US and is available on the internet, for sale in the UK.

It is an excellent visual aid for individuals to use with someone wanting to know more about what Christians believe.

Great care should be taken in using this visual aid. It should not be used indiscriminately, but only sensitively and appropriately.

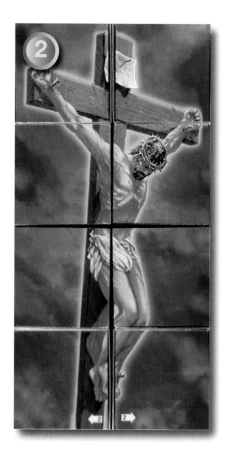

1. **'Man in sin' separated from God**
   God is perfect and loves us. He doesn't want us to perish but sin must be dealt with.

2. **Open to 'Christ on the Cross'**
   God so loved us that... John 3:16

3. **Open to the tomb**
   Men buried Jesus in a tomb. Huge stone rolled there and guards put it in place.

4. **Open to 'Risen Christ'**
   God raised Jesus from the dead. Jesus has conquered death.

5. **Open to 'Cross Bridge'**
   Jesus is the only way we can come to God. John 14:6

6. **Open to 'Heaven and Hell'**
   What choice will you make?

7. **Steps for Followers of Christ**
   (When the Evangecube is in the starting position, on the back side is this image. Use it to help the new believer grow in Christ).

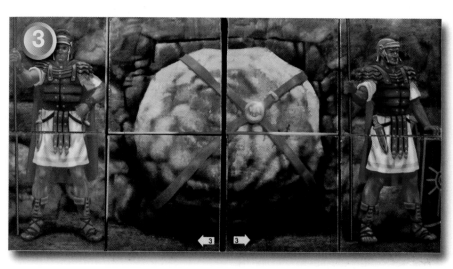

Sylvena has used the Evangecube on several occasions

An elderly gentleman watched the Evangecube being demonstrated and afterwards said that he wasn't sure that he'd be going to heaven and questioned whether you could, in fact, know that. A good discussion ensued and he later borrowed a copy of the book *How can I be sure?* by Frank Allred.

He read the book and on returning it remarked that he was certain now. The Evangecube started this whole train of events.

One day I took the large cube into the Nursing Home where I worked and asked an elderly couple if they would like to see it. The husband had had a severe stroke which left him unable to speak. He and his wife were both very interested to see the cube and the gentleman was almost tearful at the scene of Christ on the cross.

His wife was fascinated at the mechanics of it, so I left it with them for a while. On my return she told me she "had to run down to the nurses' station to share it with them." The mind boggled since she walked slowly using a frame, but she was also excited that her husband had been able to do it in the correct sequence.

It certainly brightened their day.

COMMERCIAL SUPPLIERS

EVANGECUBE

e3 Resources – £8
www.e3resources.org

Jonah's Big Fish – £5
www.jonahsbigfish.com

Deeper Shopping – £10.50
www.deepershopping.co.uk

Christian Bits – £6.81
www.christianbits.co.uk

A moving Evangecube presentation can be viewed at
www.simplysharejesus.com

PSALM 23 PUZZLE

This was designed by a gentleman in his late seventies and coloured in by a lady of a similar age.

INSTRUCTIONS TO CREATE VERSE

Photocopy this pattern – Can anyone guess what it is?

Colour each of the shapes around the circle. What does it say?

You may then like to colour in the words in a contrasting colour.

Cut out and paste onto a sheet.

You may like to include the rest of the words of the psalm underneath, and then laminate.

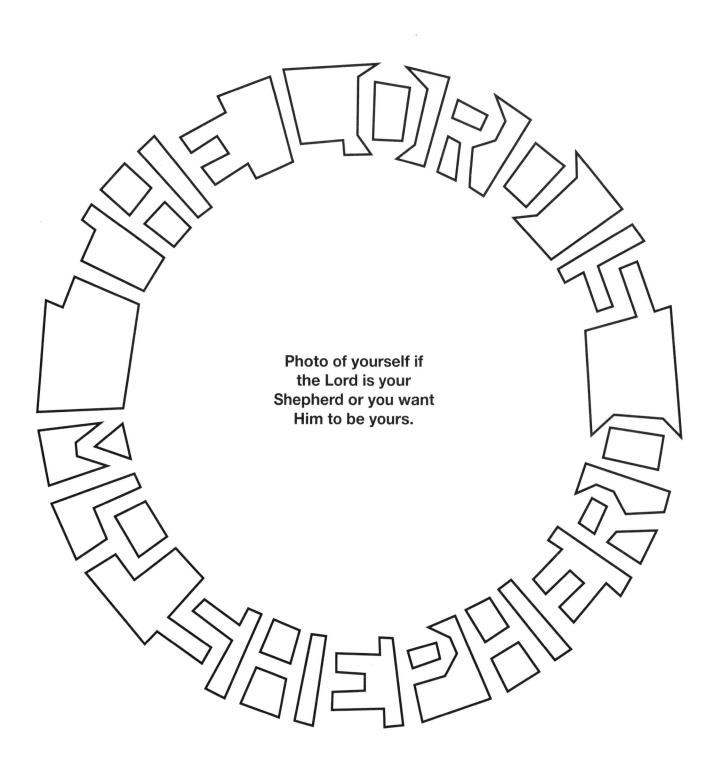

Photo of yourself if
the Lord is your
Shepherd or you want
Him to be yours.

Thoughts for talks

Psalm 23 Puzzle

The Lord is my Shepherd	RELATIONSHIP!
I shall not want	SUPPLY!
He maketh me to lie down in green pastures	REST!
He leadeth me beside still waters	REFRESHMENT!
He restoreth my soul	HEALING!
He leadeth me in paths of righteousness	GUIDANCE!
For His name's sake	PURPOSE!
Yea, though I walk through the valley of the shadow of death	CHALLENGE!
I will fear no evil	ASSURANCE!
For Thou art with me	FAITHFULNESS!
Thy rod and thy staff, they comfort me	SHELTER!
Thou preparest a table before me in the presence of my enemies	HOPE!
Thou annointest my head with oil	CONSECRATION!
My cup runneth over	ABUNDANCE!
Surely goodness and mercy shall follow me all the days of my life	BLESSING!
And I will dwell in the house of the Lord	SECURITY!
Forever	ETERNITY!

Psalm 23 (KJV)

Thoughts for talks

'God moves in a mysterious way His wonders to perform'
– it is often not until we are moving in His way that we realise where He is leading.

'As for me, the Lord has led me.' *Genesis 24:27*
How important to go where our Shepherd leads!

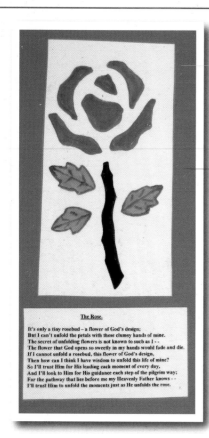

THE ROSE

It's only a tiny rosebud – a flower of God's design;

But I can't unfold the petals with these clumsy hands of mine.

The secret of unfolding flowers is not known to such as I –

The flower that God opens so sweetly in my hands would fade and die.

If I cannot unfold a rosebud, this flower of God's design,

Then how can I think I have wisdom to unfold this life of mine?

So I'll trust Him for His leading each moment of every day,

And I'll look to Him for His guidance each step of the pilgrim way;

For the pathway that lies before me my Heavenly Father knows;

I'll trust him to unfold the moments just as He unfolds the rose.

Anon